NORTH AYRSHIRE
D0523925

Start-Up Connections

FOOD AND MOVEMENT

Claire Llewellyn

Evans

Evans Brothers Limited

First published in this edition in 2010

Published by Evans Brothers Limited
2A Portman Mansions
Chiltern Street
London W1U 6NR

Produced for Evans Brothers Limited by
White-Thomson Publishing Ltd.,
+44 (0) 843 2087 460
www.wtpub.co.uk

Printed & bound in China by New Era Printing Company Limited

Editor: Dereen Taylor
Consultants: Nina Siddall, Head of Primary School Improvement, East Sussex; Norah Granger, former primary head teacher and senior lecturer in Education, University of Brighton; Kate Ruttle, freelance literacy consultant and Literacy Co-ordinator, Special Needs Co-ordinator, and Deputy Headteacher at a primary school in Suffolk.
Designer: Leishman Design
Cover design: Balley Design Limited

The right of Claire Llewellyn to be identified as the author of this work has been asserted by her in accordance with the Copyright, Designs and Patents Act 1988.

All rights reserved. No part of this publication may be reproduced, stored in a retrieval system or transmitted in any form, or by any means, electronic, mechanical, photocopying, recording or otherwise, without the prior permission of Evans Brothers Limited.

© Evans Brothers Limited 2006

British Library Cataloguing in Publication Data
Llewellyn, Claire
Forces and movement. -- (Start-up connections)
1. Force and energy--Juvenile literature. 2. Motion--Juvenile literature
I. Title II. Series
531.1-dc22

ISBN: 978 0 237 54172 9

Acknowledgements:
Special thanks to the following for their help and involvement in the preparation of this book: Staff and pupils at Elm Grove Primary School, Brighton, Liz Price and family and friends, Christine Clark and family.

Picture Acknowledgements:
Chris Fairclough Colour Library 14; Ecoscene 6, 7 *(top);* Popperfoto 7 *(bottom), 15 (bottom right);* WTPix 10. All other photographs by Chris Fairclough.

NORTH AYRSHIRE LIBRARIES
CANCELLED
05841933
Bertrams 28/03/2011
531.1 £6.99
HQ

Contents

Move that body! 4

How does it move? 6

On the move 8

Let's pull! 10

Let's push! 12

In the playground 14

Rolling along 16

Make it stop 18

Changing shape 20

Further information for Parents and Teachers 22

Index 24

Move that body!

We can move our body in all sorts of different ways.

▼ We can stretch our arms.

▲ We can swing one leg and then the other.

move body

▼ We can bend at the hips and touch our toes.

▲ We can lift one leg and balance like a dancer.

How many different parts of your body can you move?
How many different ways can you move your arms?

How does it move?

Things move in many different ways. We use all sorts of words to describe them.

▶ Look at this picture of a snake. These words describe how a snake moves.

Can you think of another animal that moves like this?

slide slither glide wriggle

How do cats and birds move?

Which of these words would you use to describe them?

flap fly jump leap

soar stalk

creep swoop

flutter

Can you move like one of these animals?

glide walk run pounce

flap swoop creep flutter pounce ...?...

On the move

Alex is getting on his scooter to find his friends in the park

▼ When he pushes his foot against the ground, the wheels turn round, and the scooter starts to move.

▲ Alex wants to go faster. He pushes his foot down harder and faster. He is moving quickly now.

pushes turn starts faster harder

▼ Alex wants to turn right now. What does he have to do?

► Alex has found his friends. How did he slow down and stop?

Let's pull!

Pulling is a way of moving things. We pull on a hat when we put it on.

▼ This water skier is being pulled along by a boat.

A pull is a kind of force. It makes things happen.

pulling force

◀ Many things in this kitchen can be pulled. How many can you spot?

What would happen if you gave this plug and these apples a pull?

Let's push!

Pushing is a way of moving things. We push open a door.

▶ We push cymbals together to make them CLASH!

▲ A push is another kind of force. It makes things happen. Look at the dominoes in this picture. What would happen if you pushed the first one?

push clash wind

Wind and running water can push things. They are forces, too.

▲ What is the force pushing this washing?

▶ What happens when Patrick puts his water wheel under the running water?

In the playground

▶ Hanif is swinging high on the swing.
It goes forward and back.

▼ Archie and his friends are on the roundabout. It's spinning round and round.

▼ Robbie and Nita are on the see-saw. It goes up and down.

How could Archie make it stop?

How are they making the see-saw move?

forward back round

How do the things in these pictures move?

up down

Rolling along

Becky and Ruth are playing skittles.

Becky rolls the ball along the ground. But she pushes the ball too gently... it does not knock the skittles down.

▶ Ruth pushes the ball much harder. The greater force makes the ball roll further. It knocks the skittles down.

rolls gently greater

▶ Morrissey rolls a marble on a carpet, on grass, on concrete, and on sand. He tries to use the same force each time. He measures how far the marble goes and writes the results on a chart. Where does the marble roll best?

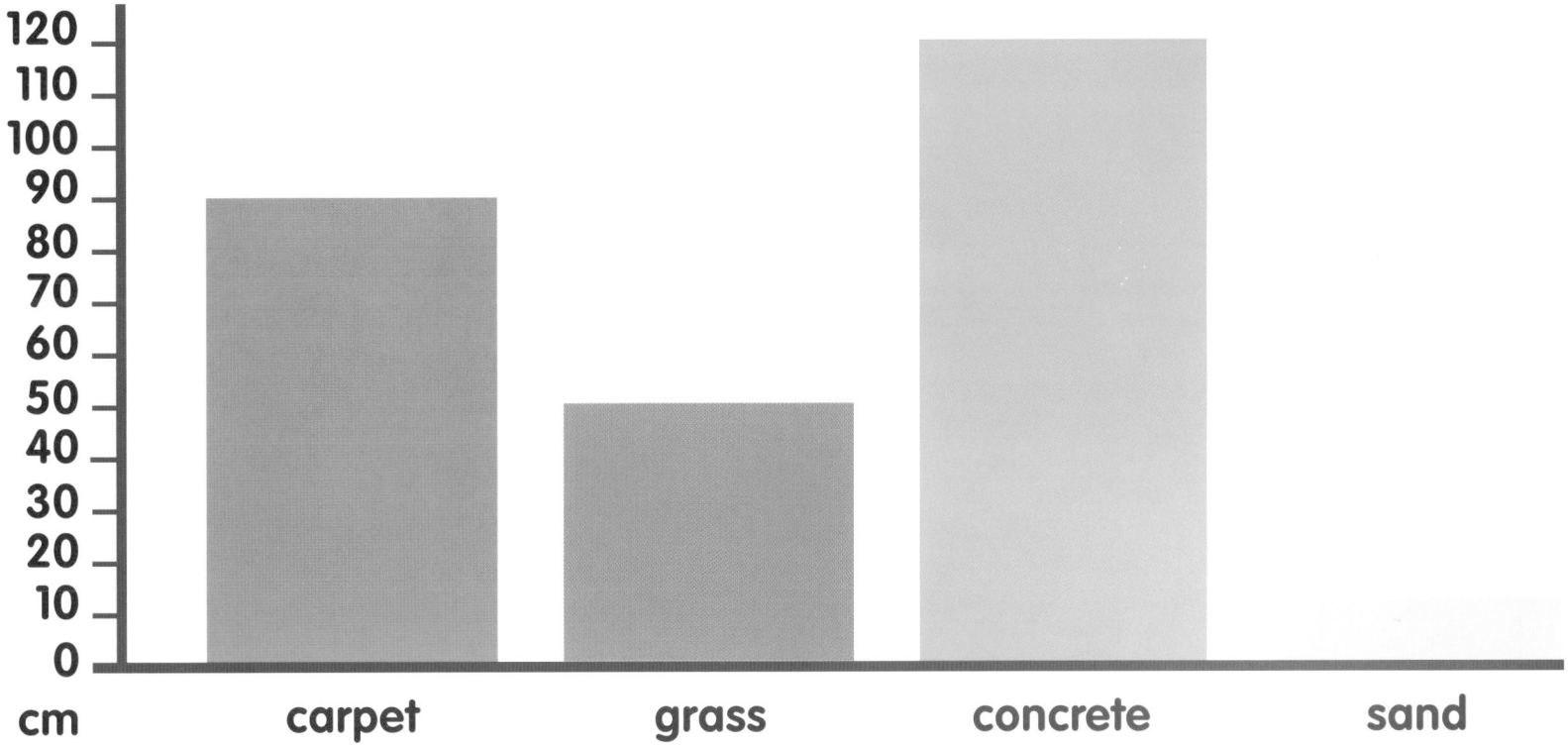

Make it stop

Tom's little sister is playing with her buggy.
The buggy rolls away.

▼ Tom pulls it back to stop it.

A force can slow things down. It can make them stop.

It is safe to stop things if they are light. It can be dangerous if they are heavy.

Which one of these two objects would you be able to stop if it were racing towards you?

Which one is too heavy?

What would happen if you tried to stop it?

Changing shape

Josh is making a snail out of play dough. He pulls and pushes the dough to **change** its **shape**.

◀ First, he makes a thin strip.

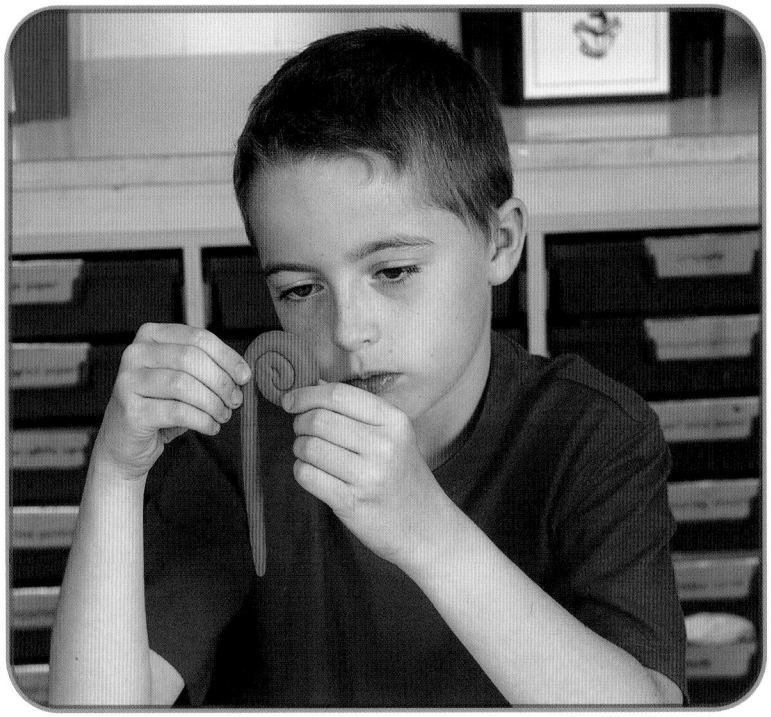

▶ Then he **curls** it to make the shell.

change shape curls

▼ He pulls off some different-coloured dough to make the body. How does he make the horns?

▲ Latha is making a long, wriggly worm. Her worm might **break** in two. Do you know why?

Further information for Parents and Teachers

FORCES AND MOVEMENT ACTIVITY PAGE

Use the activities on these pages to help you to make the most of *Forces and Movement* in your classroom.

Activities suggested on this page support progression in learning by consolidating and developing ideas from the book and helping the children to link the new concepts with their own experiences. Making these links is crucial in helping young children to engage with learning and to become lifelong learners.

Ideas on the next page develop essential skills for learning by suggesting ways of making links across the curriculum and in particular to science, numeracy and ICT.

WORD PANEL

Check that the children know the meaning of each of these words from the book.

backward	faster	joint	roll
balance	finish	movement	slower
bend	force	pull	start
change	forward	push	stretch

DEVELOPING VOCABULARY

Take children to the hall to explore different ways of moving.

- Establish their basic vocabulary of speed and direction: *forwards, backwards, sideways, fast, quickly, slow, push, pull.*
- Can they walk in different ways: *tiptoe, stride, stumble, stamp, creep, stagger, trip, plod, trudge, sneak, pace, saunter?* And can they *dance, hop, skip, run, race, sprint, hurry, speed, dash?* Talk about why people move in these ways and what each tells us about how people are feeling.
- Introduce names of animals and ask children to move like the animals. Develop their vocabulary of words to describe how the animals can move.

MOVING CHILDREN

Explore how the children's own bodies move. They can work in pairs to watch each other move and observe directions and kinds of movement. If you have any children in the class with physical disabilities, use your knowledge of your children to determine which activities are appropriate.

- How many places in their bodies can they bend? Are all of the bends in the same direction?
- How many places in their bodies can they roll? Do all of these places roll in the same direction and to the same degree?
- Ask them to think about how their bodies would be different if they couldn't, for example, bend their knees or arms at all and if their thumbs just bent like their other fingers.

MOVING TOYS

Either collect toys from around the school, or ask children to bring in toys from home - including toys for younger siblings.

- Give children opportunities to explore a range of toys, trying to find out everything that they can do. (You may need to remind children about respecting the toys so that they are not tested to destruction.)
- Children can take photos of the toys using digital cameras. They can then annotate the pictures with symbols to indicate how the toys move.
- Ask children to consider which forces they had to use to make each of the toys move: *push, pull, twist, press, slide, roll, turn, lift* They can add the new information to their annotations.

CARING MOVEMENTS

Read books which show caring relationships, both between children and from adult to child. Use the pictures to identify movements and forces which are associated with caring relationships. Be sensitive to, and prepare for, the possibility of safeguarding disclosures.

- Give children copies of the books, as well as pictures showing caring relationships. Identify movements which are associated with these relationships and the contexts (eg pushing a pushchair, clapping, hugging)
- Recognise uncaring relationships and identify movements which are associated with them (eg pushing someone over, hitting, squeezing)
- Discuss the idea that we can use our bodies for both kinds of relationships. Make reference to the school rules and focus more on caring relationships.

USING FORCES AND MOVEMENT FOR CROSS CURRICULAR WORK

The revised national curriculum focuses on children developing key competencies as

- successful learners
- confident individuals and
- responsible citizens.

Cross curricular work is particularly beneficial in developing the thinking and learning skills that contribute to building these competencies because it encourages children to make links, to transfer learning skills and to apply knowledge from one context to another. As importantly, cross curricular work can help children to understand how school work links to their daily lives. For many children, this is a key motivation in becoming a learner.

The web below indicates some areas for cross curricular study. Others may well come from your own class's engagement with the ideas in the book.

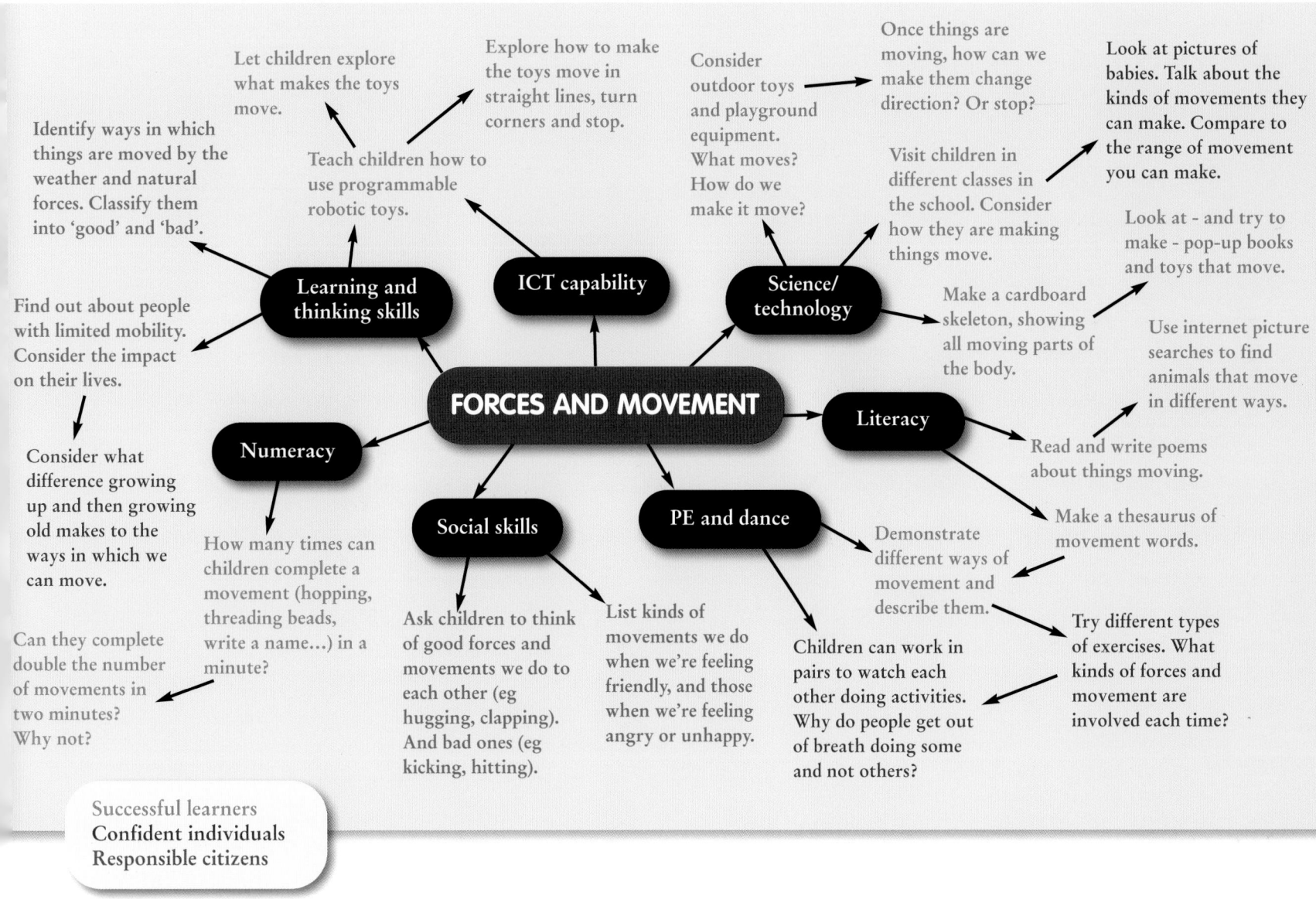

Index

a

animal movements 6, 7

b

balancing 5

bending 5

boat 10

body movements 4, 5, 6, 7

c

changing shapes 20, 21

f

forces 10, 12, 13, 16, 17, 18

m

moving faster 8

moving forwards and back 14, 15

p

pulling 10, 11, 18, 20, 21

pushing 8, 12, 13, 16, 20

r

rolling 16, 17, 18

roundabout 14

s

scooter 8, 9

see-saw 14

skittles 16

slowing down 9, 18

spinning 14

starting 8

stopping 9, 14, 18, 19

stretching 4

swing 14

swinging 4, 14

t

turning 8, 9

w

water 13

water skier 10

water wheel 13

wind 13